Stay Alive

Written by Oshri Liron Hakak
Illustrated by Andrea Ceballos García

BUTTERFLYON BOOKS

Stay Alive

Written by Oshri Liron Hakak and Illustrated by Andrea Ceballos García

Published by Butterflyon Books

Los Angeles

ISBN 978-1-7349790-6-0

To anyone who doesn't feel like being here, now.

Stay alive.
Because flowers...

... and because sunshine...

... and also mountains and the beach.

Plus, animals.

Friends and hugs, too.
Hugs and friends yet unmet...
at least one or two wait ahead, I bet.

Great conversations still await
you ahead, with guidance to
hear and guidance to share.
Also, sitting.

There's also the wonderful release
of going pee, probably.

So even if you're not feeling so lively...
stay alive.

Eventually the pain might fit on a shelf?
Maybe near the tea or the cookie elf?

And if you don't have a shelf,
maybe one day you will.

For now you can put it in
a pocket or a pouch,
next to some cool rocks or leaves—
even while your heart heals and grieves.

I almost forgot...
you have some breaths
and heartbeats, too.

These can help to steer you through,
and when it looks
like your options are fewer than two,
you may find new ways through
that you never knew you knew.

You've got breaths to come that can open worlds of possibility and release the stuff that's yucky and goopy.

Some heartbeats that can fuel
the planting of new gardens and great
forests of wonder and Love...
or forests of actual trees.

And music!
You might make some or listen,
they are equally important.

So stay with us.

Because if you study the weather,
you'll notice no storm lasts forever...

And things get better.

So feel what you feel
as a tree feels a drought before rain,
or as the moon feels the darkness
of its monthly wane.

Whoever you are
and wherever you are...
know that you are loved.

You are precious to me.
I'm here for you.
I love you.

THE BEND

Thank you...

Thanks for reading this little nook of a book.
Feel free to read it again... especially because
I forgot to write in the beginning that it is best
read with lots of slow-deep-breathiness and
potentially some tiny smileyness.
So try that if you want, k?

45

P.S. Because, you know, you've got so much to live for... just FYI. I know that because everyone's at least got some tiny things, and tiny things are huge. Like songs you want to hear or make, pictures you want to see or create, grains of sand or clods of dirt you want to explore, or steadfast boogers that call for picking.

46

Some resources...

47

If you or someone you know is in need of support, there are people here to help. Contact the National Suicide Prevention Lifeline 24 hours a day, 7 days a week from anywhere in the United States.

National Suicide Prevention Lifeline
1-800-273-8255
SuicidePreventionLifeline.org

As of July, 2022, you may also dial 988 to connect you with the National Suicide Prevention Lifeline.

For outside the US, please visit findahelpline.com

Keep in touch...

You can find more of Andrea's art on Instagram at @andreakushisha and Oshri's on Instagram at @oshrihakak and ButterflyonBooks.com, as well as the music of Brock Pollock, who contributed creatively to the writing of this book, on Instagram at @brockpollock.